The House in my Head

Rachael Mathew

BookLeaf Publishing

Presentation by *BookLeaf Publishing*

Web: www.bookleafpub.com

E-mail: info@bookleafpub.com

ISBN: 9789358311297

First edition 2023

I wake up…

Inside a disco ball at the start of each day
A thousand mirrors magnify my scars and dark
colors
Obscuring any view of the doorway
This is going to be a long summer

My dad left town four years ago
Yet his records still play on a loop in the storage
room
The older I get, the more his voice seems to
grow
As a million mirrors echo what he assumed

So I rest my head on a pillow stuffed with
daydreams
As the lemon tea on the kitchen counter grows
cold
But the pages of every fantasy novel seem
To taste better than the sour truth a billion
mirrors hold

I stare at myself in trillion fun house mirrors,
hoping to find one palatable.
My once rosy cheeks have become stubs.

Do I have to cut my nose to make every room I
enter habitable?
I hide away and grow gray but never grow up.

"I'll wake up soon, I promise."
But my bubble made of glass will shatter
before I can ever be honest

My father: the neighbor who moved away four years ago

My neighbor had generations-old trauma
along with a cracked wedding band
On his front lawn.

When I moved to town with a lawn as expansive
as the White House,
My neighbor finally had a place to dump 33
years of garbage.
"It'll turn your grass into an emerald sea just like
mine," he said
While vultures ate away at my dried, wilting
white lilacs.

I stood there while my knuckles turned white
While the sealed kettle on my stove shot steam
While a leaning tower of greasy crumb-filled
dishes defied gravity
While the clogged sink brimmed with water
But when I was 18, I stepped on a branch, and it
snapped

So I turned my windowless basement into my
neighbor's new home

By now, his black hair must be peppered with
silver and grey streaks
And a fly trap's jaw must rust when its sunshine
is behind a locked door

But instead, he yells obscenities from the crack
of dawn.
I'd rather smell rotting flesh from six feet under
than have the world's worst alarm clock.

The woman in the windowless house

My lawn was my father's choice for a landfill.
Bricks were thrown, and broken glass on my
window sill.
In my neighborhood, there was also a
windowless house.
I'd pound on its doors, crying to my father's
spouse.

The woman would sip hot lemon tea
And plug her nose from the debris.
"Rachael, please, just lock your doors."
"Just brush the shattered glass under your
floors."

My father skipped town when my grass turned
brown and scorched.
But I finally started seeing his wife on her front
porch.
Maybe I'd finally learn this woman's name.
Maybe I could finally fill 18 years of empty
picture frames.

October 17th, 2020

You asked to come inside, and I tentatively
agreed
We ate pizza on ice coolers as you moved closer
to me
I was a deer in headlights; you had an angelic
glow
Your foot's on the gas; we didn't want to take it
slow

You wanted to outline my body on my bed
without covers
In the movies, this is how two strangers become
lovers
You picked white lilacs that arose from the
cracks of my asphalt skin
No one had chosen to walk down my street
before, so I took it on the chin

You promised me you'd grow them in your
garden
But when the lights turn on, my naiveness has
been bargained
Stems clenched in your gripped fist like a trophy
Are your other teenage conquests displayed
below me?

Three years passed, and I'm still trapped in my
bed like it's a gurney
I add posters to white hospital walls and don't
let my hair grow
I spend hundreds on blue pills, stoic doctors, and
therapy
Because a 24-year-old didn't want to take it slow

Moving out and moving on

God, please, don't let tonight be the night that I
slip
Into the front door of a boy I've tried to erase
from my mind.
Whose name, when mentioned, is followed by a
couple of whiskey sips.
You're my last call; every other has declined.

The car keys on the dining table are more
convincing than history

The rose-colored glasses are more tempting in
my greyscale world
The warmth of his arms is more persuading in
my misery
Our love story can't be rewritten with a different
girl

It's been two and a half months since he tore
himself from me.
Muscle memory brings me to his apartment.
Sitting on Presidential Road behind the willow
tree,
Where we threw out a batch of cookie dough
because we forgot the parchment.

He's careful about who he lets in, but his door's
ajar.
I'm met with naked hardwood floors and a
blanket of dust.
Thinking I've entered a stranger's apartment, I
turn back to the car.
But I see wrinkled white lilacs on the floor with
browned edges like rust.

I heard he moved to the land of palm trees and
CEOs.
I still dance to his records even after the music
ends.

There's now an Infinite Loop of blue suits in his
closet instead of used clothes.
I'm wasting my pennies on him, hoping they'll
land on heads.

God, please, distract me from my delusion.
It's been three years since a 19-year-old chose to
be stuck in the past.
But I'll go back and forth like a pendulum till I
reach a conclusion
On whether crumpled lilacs can be regrown or
thrown in the trash.

Prodigal daughter

Scrolling for hours hypnotized by blue light
Drunk without alcohol, how much time have I
abused?
Seeing those who have less but are achieving
more,
Is like pushing a thumb into my bruise.

Am I undeserving of the parent I have?
Do I have too much, is that why I gain so little?
Like the prodigal son, I have a house I can
always return to.
If success is just a choice, I'll take the blue pill in
this riddle.

But if I could enter and exit book covers,
Dress up as the fairest stepdaughter in the whole
city,

Why would I need to grow callouses on my
fingers,
When I could live in the universe in my mind
like Walter Mitty?

Two-way street

There's a beautiful boy on my bus today
He wears black clothes, a scarf he knit
And a star around his neck that's grey
What's his last name? I'd like to have it.

He lives a stone's throw away from me
I fantasize about sneaking out my back door
Tiptoeing in the dark through the trees
Drunk on lust in my veins, I want more

Tonight's the night I bite the bullet.
I start the walk to him on a positive note.
Though I'm cold in this summer outfit,
he'll meet me halfway and offer me his coat.

I've been walking for fourteen minutes.
He's bound to walk up the path
Oh, I hear a scuffle! Not it's just crickets
Will he be the one to end my wrath?

I reach his apartment, shivering to my bones
But his lights are off, there's no one to greet
In the lamplight, I see I've been walking this
path alone
On a single road, not a two-way street.

I saw a boy on the bus today
I sat across from him, and he looked at me like I
was glass
We're passengers on a sinking ship floating
separate ways
Dear love, you are a complete ass.

Gori Gori, Gorgeous

I spend hours in a dimly lit home, staring at a
clock.
Curtains block the warm yellow rays from the
coast
As rust forms on my front door lock
And I turn pale like a ghost.

"Am I the fairest in all the land?" each day I ask
and bother.
Whose eyes do I see in the magic mirror?
Those of every man from the same land as my
father.
They once belonged to a guileless girl, but I can
no longer hear her.

Keys to the Kingdom

I was thirteen sitting in your backseat yesterday.
It's a bad dream I've been shaking off for 9
years.
You're throwing daggers at my face like it's
child's play.
But you say "tough love" works, and I'll only
learn to fly if I'm pushed off a pier.

My childhood ended when I thought a BBQ fork
could make me disappear like a magic trick.
Why was I curled in the corner to become your
punching bag? I've got no clue.
Did God tell you to beat me with a stick?
Or is that how your father said, "I love you"?

You turned my blue skies into ceilings of
enclosed captivity.
You needed a project and held the keys to my
cage, Dad.
I was disconnected from Earth, on a spaceship
without life or gravity
But you were the only home I ever had.

I'm now twenty-two sitting in the driver's seat;
you still have the largest artillery.

I'm moving to a house five hours away from
Massachusetts.
You tell me about the dangers of Philly and my
financial irresponsibility,
Acting pharisaical to mask years of neglect and
impudence.

If I hadn't stayed all these years, imagine what I
could've achieved.
But I've got keys to my own kingdom now.
Oh darling, are you sad to see me leave?
The act is over; take a bow.

The boy with the fake name

A little crumb of your attention is like a
three-layered cake.
My eyelids grow heavy, but my heart has not
Forgotten what you told me in your dark room
on Thanksgiving break,
"Rachael, you're the greatest friend I've got."

So I'll sit by the window, my true love, my real
love
Watching the puffy prom dresses in limousines
become wedding dresses
I'll sit by the window waiting for my true love,
my real love
You're the only song I'll sing on repeat; you take
all my yesses

I'm waiting for you to re-ignite that dying flame
in me, my love
I put a boiling cup of lemon tea to my lips and
don't even flinch
I'm waiting for you to write the rest of my
forty-two-page story, love
You're my broken record, and I'm spiraling in
the grooves inch by inch

Did I say something that turned your face away
from mine?
Why was I your last resort when you were my
only exception?
Was my table not set properly? Did you want
more expensive wine?
Or is there nothing I can do to change your
perception?

I'm eager, like a child, to be a pawn in your
chess game.
Into the lion's den, smiling ear to ear like a
baboon.
But you never wanted to know my name,
You just wanted to touch someone one Thursday
afternoon.

Collecting skins like a hunter, where will I be
displayed?
My hobbies, my poems, my voice can't get you
high like a cigarette.
So I'll trade my boundaries for fool's gold that'll
rust in a day
Because lust is the best kind of love I'll ever get.

Lust is the best kind of love I'll ever get.

Your name means "one with a real appearance."
But I won't turn you into the penile system.

Because even though you're a con artist,
I'm your favorite helpless little victim.

Window Shopping

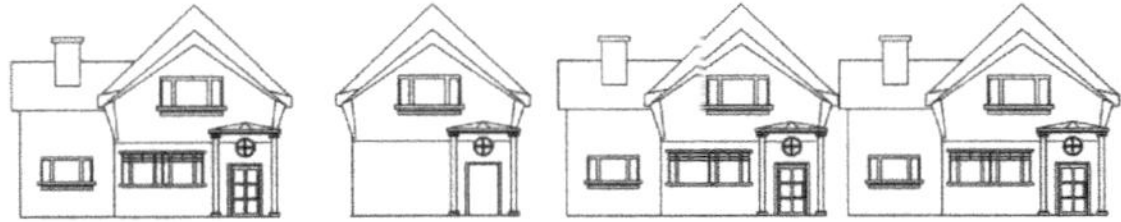

Today, I sit on the curb and window shop.
I know, I promised to budget, but everyone's
drinking this white wine.
In just three weeks, seven pounds can be
dropped!
I only have money for dinner tonight, but there's
only one left. This has to be a sign!

When the Johnsons are playing their nightly
Yahtzee, I take out my wine
And dance to no music in front of my living
room window.
From outside, my living room looks like a
ballroom, spacious enough to have a Congo line.
But that metallic dress for my new figure costs
hundreds
So I've sold my couches and heirloom pendant
shaped like a minnow.

But if I wear vintage Versace in my home that's
pre-owned,

What would the Walters say? Would they report
a robbery?
They finally started inviting me to their cocktail
parties. Could I now get disowned?
It'd cost an arm to rebuild this home, but it's
better than dealing with their snobbery.

The builders prove my doubts right and tell me
it'll cost an extra two grand
"The whole town's filled with plastic doll
houses."
"We're trying to preserve those that have been
for decades on this land."
So I sold my hair, and until I can afford a wig,
I'll be as stealthy as a mouse.

As my doors, aged with peeling paint,
indecipherable crayon doodles, and high school
crushes' initials, are swapped
With shiny, hollow walls stamped with a serial
number,
I sit on my curb and window shop
To find which neighbor I'll vicariously live
through today.
Because without trends and champagne drama,
where can my attention be paid?

I've had to reheat my lemon tea 12 times now

Before drinking my nightly lemon tea, I check
all the locks six times like clockwork.
Because how can you get a good look at them in
the dim kitchen lighting the first four times?
At Sarah's weekend cocktail parties, I tell people
this is my fun quirk.
Call me careworn, but even the Hills have been
known to have pilfered crimes.

Haven't you thought about someone breaking in
and stealing a vintage heirloom or those Asiago
bagels you paid an extra three dollars for?
And maybe the someone stealing your Asiago
bagels is Sarah, whom you told at last weekend's
party that you were going gluten-free because
you didn't want to try her free-range grass-fed
homemade walnut bread 'made with love'?
And maybe now Sarah feels vengeful and
decides to explore more of your pantry and finds
the jar of strawberry jam left unopened as
though it was purchased yesterday and not gifted
two years ago as her birthday present to you in
which she drove to her local strawberry field

three hours away to handpick every ounce of
sweetness?

What if, with all this snooping and betrayal,
Sarah's gotten quite hungry and decides to snack
on an Asiago bagel saturated in gluten with a
spread of the fruits of her labor (strawberry jam,
to be specific) but when she looks into the
cutlery cupboard she doesn't find any knives so
she decides to check every drawer of your home
for knives and she finally finds them along with
a pack of cotton balls in your bedroom desk
drawer?

And what if she remembers that you said you get
cold easily when she asked why you always
wear long sleeves?

And what if that night you only checked the
locks twelve times?

Shirking: My nomadic lifestyle

I pack up my house the instant I arrive
To the sprawling green lawns of Lexington,
And the Amherst dorms students swarm like a
beehive.
Maybe I should instead visit the crystal blue
rivers of Kingston?

I'm a broken puzzle piece trying to find a corner
I fit into,
So my passport becomes the size of a dictionary.
At first, the houses that look like crooked teeth
seem edgy and new
Then the sparkles get blinding, and a picturesque
lifestyle seems less visionary

So I pack up my house and move to a different
town.
I fill my rooms with neighborhood welcome
parties instead of dust
But I can't shake the feeling that I'm being
followed around
By the holes in my childhood bedroom walls,
I'm nonplussed.

I blame the streetlights for the obstructed view
out my window.
Instead of washing the sky-high dishes piling in
my sink.
I keep packing up my house as my
accountability plays limbo.
I'll wait on the porch for a savior, sipping my
lemon drink.

First person to Antarctica

First. As a child, I despised that this was how I
was defined.
So my parents became my older siblings in my
mind.
But I was Eve living in a paradise and the first to
taste the fruit of a karaka.
I was a pioneer venturing to the world's frozen
underbelly, Antarctica

I was the first to wear a rainbow flag, the first in
therapy, the firstborn.
There's no roadmap to guide me through life's
eternal winter storm
I can't tell where North is, and I'm in poor
condition
Will there be anything for me to show at the end
of this expedition?

My mother's forehead is marked with lines of
concern.
Faded streamers for when her daughter makes
her triumphant return.
Her husband cries loudly in church pews rather
than with his family commune,

But mother holds the only sanctuary each of her
three children has, like a triune.

Will the seeds my mother has sown in me turn
into millions?
Am I a lighthouse for my siblings, or will the
distance make us strangers, civilians?
I sink into the snow each time I see those who
are miles ahead of me.
But how quickly I forget the thought of leaving
my hometown was once a pipe dream.

Groundhog's Day

I awake each morning in a home that looks like
a graveyard
I even see it grinning like Cheshire for just a
flash
Every morning, my doubts get proven right
again and again
This broken record can't be unscratched

Every door I open seems to be slammed in my
face
My tears can't dissolve what has already
hardened
I end up re-living the same story again and again
No matter how much I try to turn a ghost town
into a garden

Men with peppered hair and the indentation of a
ring on their finger,
Smile and look into my eyes so I show them an
inch.
At night, my undefiled skin their crimson paint
mars.
In the morning, I find a child with eyes like mine
and skin cold to the touch.
My home's become a graveyard.

The (attempted) escape

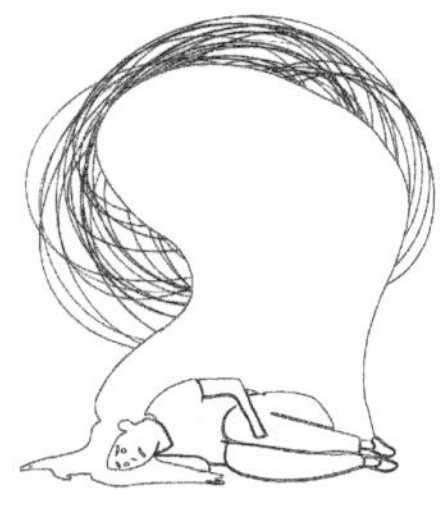

Mommy, Mommy!
Please let me out!
I can't be here anymore!
Please don't make me sleep in my room!
There's a monster living under my floors!
He sleeps inside my eyelids! He tickles my ears!
I can't be here anymore!
He has a billion books in his library and never
stops to take a breath
To read me bedtime stories, but they never put
me to sleep.
They make me feel frozen, like a popsicle in the
freezer.
Each one ends with you throwing a birthday
party in our backyard while I sleep under a dirt
floor.

Aren't you going to wake me up? Haven't you
noticed my empty chair? Don't you hear my
pounding under the floorboards?

Please don't make me sleep another night.
I can't breathe here anymore.

The termites

I can hear you whispering from under the floor.
I'm tired of being vigilant.
You enjoy breaking me, God's silliest little
experiment.
So I'll become your step stool.
"The most submissive girl you ever fooled."
Being a traveling pastor has become mundane;
you want to change the script.
So I'll become the gasoline for your power trip.
Here, take this Catechumen oil and douse this
entire home.
Invite all your friends to take a bite out of me
and turn me into an empty dome.
Crawl into every corner and crevice, don't let my
discomfort stop you.
Preaching chastity at the pulpit, but I'm your
favorite taboo.
I deserve damnation for seducing your virtuous
spirit.
A forty-three-year-old was tempted by a
sixteen-year-old being promiscuous.

After you've pleasured yourself, bury me alive.

Don't worry; no blue and red lights are coming;
even my dad agrees there's been no heinous
crime.
But isn't it going to be tough to write your
sermon on the book of Jeremiah,
While you can hear me crying on the bathroom
floor to your Messiah?

When your nails are covered in dirt and blood,
Just remember that six feet of dirt can't conceal
the poundings
Of a child you forced into becoming a woman.

Are you satisfied now?
Are you satisfied now?
Are you satisfied now?
Are you satisfied now?

20 years from now, they'll excavate my body to
find
My insides have been eaten away by termites,
just like the wooden beams of my home.
My clothing's completely destroyed, but your
name will never be made known.

The rescue

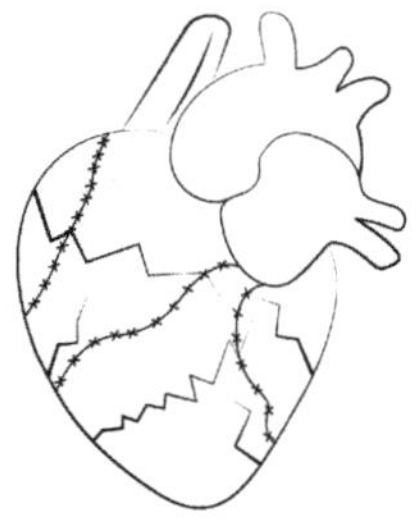

You called to ask if I'm using the fresh linens
you bought.
But I'm not singing the same song.
I'm choking on tears trying not to scream.
You keep asking me what's wrong,
As I'm holding a lit match outside my house
that's covered in gasoline.

You drive for hours till midnight with two small
headlights
Trying to find sanity on a thickly wooded
twisted path,
Before you lose yours in my self-destructive
plight.
But isn't all revenge best served with a side of
fire and ash?

You pull up in the driveway, breath caught in
your chest.
But you release a sigh when you see an
unflamed house and me curled in a ball.
Heedfulness disrupted my departure plans. I
didn't prepare for guests.
Jealously eroded my kingdom, but you won't let
me end up like Saul.
You don't ask a single question and walk into the
house.
You wet a washcloth and wipe the walls down.
You cut up fresh apples and wash my oil-stained
blouse.
You plant a hyssop plant into the ground.

Maybe it was guilt or ego, but I felt like a child
in a high chair.
So you received all my stubborn remarks, cold
shoulders, and slammed doors.
Until one day, you called me up to ask if I got
my flat tire repaired,
As I heard an angry man in the background
smashing a plate on the floor.

For four years, I've been your first thought in the
morning and your last call at night.
My burdens are heavy, but your crown of
motherhood is made of lead.

Your house is built on sand and is teaming with
termites.
Folding my fresh linens is a refuge away from
the home in your head.

Art out of the dark

The doorknob to my basement grows with dust.
If I do enter it, it's only for minutes at a time.
When guests arrive, I seem as tidy as a news presenter.
But down there, I've stuffed every insult thrown my way and petty crime.

What is the point of the scars 'loved ones" have branded me with,
If not taken as a lesson and turned into stars?
How can I pretend a whole room of my house doesn't exist,
When it's the one thing that inspired me to turn my pen into a jaguar?

I want to blow the dust off of every bloody knife in that basement,
And place it on a lit stage or glass-cased in a museum, undefiled.
Not to have my face stamped on the front of Time Magazine,
But to become the lending hand I needed as a child.

Those rickety basement stairs are etched with
my history and DNA,
I start spiraling before finding a sliver of light
and inspiration.
But if I can't find atonement through the pain
life's brought me,
Can becoming an artist be my true declaration?

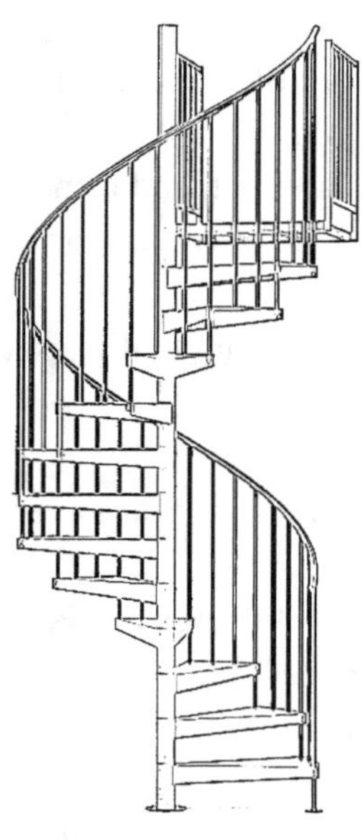

Mrs. Delilah the Daydreamer

A woman on my block paces for hours in her
bedroom.
Can you see her through the slits of her window
blinds?
She thinks she's being inconspicuous,
But her every step the downstairs neighbors
despise.

She reads books all day from her invisible
library.
Sometimes getting too involved in a hero's
journey is so compelling,
She'll stub her toe against her metal bed frame.
But she doesn't miss a beat in her storytelling.

She hasn't read aloud these pages to anyone
She's even got her room rigged with burglar
alarms
It's not because people will stain or steal those
pristine white pages.
But they'll laugh that she treats fairytales like a
Bible, not a lucky charm.

These books started as her bedtime stories at
five years old.

Now they're the only thing stopping her from
becoming a worm's next meal.
She won't buy new books, just changes the
characters' names.
Regardless, her door hinges, now coated in rust,
are sealed.

The last lullaby

I walk towards you in the dark with my head
down.
I see you waiting at the front door steps
With your golden smile and brown frizzy hair.
You ask me what's wrong, but in that instant, I
forget.

Out of all the glittering watches and the
Rapunzels, I'm on your arm.
You're a magnet for all the eyes at the ball, but
you seem distracted by me.
Why would the track athlete go for the
bookworm with slouchy clothes?
But you ask, "Will you have this dance, my
lady?"

The sun starts peeking through the pearly
ballroom curtains.
My dear, kiss me in front of the world before the
sand in my hourglass ends!
I don't want to wake up to a life behind a locked
bedroom door
And find that my loneliness has created you and
this dress, blue and gemmed!
No, I'm not ready to leave yet!

Just one more second of believing a lie!
Just one more second of being alive!
Please don't wake me up!
Please don't wake me up!
Please don't wake me-